Choices

The Young Black Man's Guide to Successful Living

Choices

The Young Black Man's Guide to Successful Living

Matthew C. Horne

Optimum Success International Publishing
Fort Washington, MD

Optimum Success International
Post Office Box 441328
Fort Washington, MD 20744-4109

Orders@matthewchorne.com

http://www.matthewchorne.com

The author of this book provides information for attaining success and living your best life possible. The provided information is based on the personal philosophy of the author. The intent is to offer general information that, when applied, will aid the reader in his quest for maximizing his human potential and self-discovery. In the event that you use any of the information in this book, the author and publisher assume no responsibility for your actions.

Printed in the United States of America

ISBN 978-0-9794550-2-5

Dedication

This book is dedicated to the most influential black male in my life: my father, Bernard Horne. He showed me that struggles are never final if we exercise our power to create the change we desire. I'm thankful to him for showing me how to always create opportunities for myself, and never be afraid to go after what I want from life. My father epitomizes the words of famed motivational speaker Willie Jolley: "A setback is a setup for a comeback!" Thank you, Bernard Horne, for making me fearless.

Table of Contents

Preface

With the overwhelming negative imagery that pervades the audio and digital airwaves, there exists the need to change the young black man's perception of himself. The objective of *Choices: The Young Black Man's Guide to Successful Living* is to paint a picture of possibility in the minds of our young black men. The focus of this work is to concentrate on the many young black males who have "made it" in society, most notably one of the most audacious young black males in history: President Barack Obama.

Throughout the book, I chronicle my childhood choices that allowed me to receive a full basketball scholarship at a Division I university, and to become the author of four books by the age of twenty-eight. I use my life experiences in a nonbraggadocious manner to paint the picture of what's possible for any black male if he consciously develops a vision for his life.

Vision is the overwhelming theme throughout this book, as this is the main ingredient in the life of any innovator, high-achiever, or successful person. The examples of possibility for young black males are real throughout this book as I chronicle growing up in a house where my father battled drug addiction, which consequently led to a single-parent household for many of my young years. My father beat the addiction once and for all when I was six years old, imbedding in my mind that any adverse circumstance is never final unless we declare it to be. My youth was not a straight path to success. It was littered with bad decisions that had me going nowhere fast, but ultimately I made choices that rescued me from a questionable lifestyle. Choices are what allowed me to take a turn with my life at a young age, positioning me to live my dreams of playing Division I basketball and receiving a free college education.

The power of "choice" is exposed as the key to changing any unfavorable circumstance young black men may find themselves in. Young black males will be empowered by the reading of this book, as they will know in their core that anything is possible for their lives. The power to create their life, their way is exposed with every turn of the page.

Chapter 1: The Power of Vision

A man is nothing without a vision in life that is fueled by a sense of purpose. The vision that you create for your life will ultimately determine where you land. A man must not just create a vision for his life, but also find the power to do what it takes to make the vision a reality. Average people meander through life, going with the flow of whatever comes their way. This book is intended to introduce you to your greatness.

A great man not only creates a vision for his life; he never stops moving forward toward it until it is accomplished.

What I mean by "vision" is creating a clear picture of where you'd like your life to go. You are the architect of your life; the vision you create is usually the one you will find yourself living in. Everyone has a vision in life, believe it or not. You may ask: what is the vision of the man whose life is impoverished and he lives a life where he can't see beyond where his next high will come from? The answer: living in poverty and getting high is his vision, which becomes his reality as his life wastes away.

Whatever vision consumes you is the one you will take steps toward on a daily basis.

You may not have been aware of the fact that you already have a vision for your life, even while reading these words. Check your daily habits and the outcomes they continuously create, and there you have it: that is your vision.

Vision is birthed on the inside. Growing up as a young black man in Prince George's County, Maryland, I couldn't always control the circumstances around me. My upbringing was far from picture-perfect, as I grew up in a house in which my father battled drug addiction until I was six years old. I remember taking trips with my family to rehabs to see my father. I also have vivid memories of having to move temporarily to my grandmother's house, as circumstances became too grave to live in at times with my father battling addiction. I can even remember when my father had to move back in with his mother in an attempt to get his life in order, and him telling me at five years old that I was "the man of the house."

This was a circumstance that I physically could not escape as an adolescent, because I was at the mercy of my parents for shelter and overall survival. I could escape it mentally and choose to create a vision for my life that was the polar opposite of what my young eyes witnessed on a daily basis.

Sometimes in life, circumstances are circumstances. They are beyond your ability to change in that moment, but creating a larger picture in your mind of what's possible for you allows circumstances not to confine you. A vision is nothing more than a reality you wish to live in. Your current situation does not have to be your reality when you possess the ability to create a vision and take steps toward that being your reality.

As I approached my teenage years, I began to make some of the same decisions my father made as a youngster that were responsible for him struggling with his drug addiction. By the grace of God, my father, once and for all, defeated addiction and was able to move back in with my family. When my dad saw me hanging out in the neighborhood with questionable people, he would get out of his car and demand that I come with him. At the time, I just thought he was being unreasonable. They were just my friends. And yes, they may have been considerably older, and into some questionable behaviors, but I saw them as nothing but cool people for me to kick it with. He saw the big picture. He recalled his days of hanging out in his neighborhood with people participating in activities that ultimately led to an addiction for the larger portion of his life. When he said, "Get into the car," in a manner in which I could only say a quick good-bye and then get into the car, this was his love saying, "I refuse to let you go down the same path I did. I know you're young, but you see firsthand where this life has led me and the difficulty it has brought our family." "Get in the car" meant: go in the opposite direction of the hardships that await bad decisions and bad surroundings.

Oftentimes in life, our vision does not go beyond our surroundings. My dad was attempting to give me a fighting chance in life, as I am to you. I am saying to you today: get in the car! If you have questionable surroundings and associates based on your less than smart choices, you have a chance to "get in the car."

The path my father's life took was a thought I always kept in the back of my mind when I was hanging out with questionable people. Those days when my dad pulled up, I got in the car. But then there were other times when he had to come and look for me when I was up to no good. It's almost as if he had radar or some sort of sixth sense that would always allow him to find me. His attempts may have seemed like they were going nowhere, as I kept hanging out and doing whatever I wanted to do, but each attempt was letting me know how serious the outcomes my dad saw for my life, which I couldn't see, actually were.

I did my share of stupid stuff growing up. I put myself in situations where I easily could have been arrested and caught, criminal cases that would still be on my record today. I found myself being chased by authorities and getting away by a hair, and probably avoided more situations than I'm even aware of.

When you live the fast life, there's usually someone watching you and counting on your misstep to catch you in a vulnerable position.

By the grace of God, I was able to find my way out of that life before I got in too deep.

The Life Preserver

My saving grace came when I was thirteen years old. I had just fractured my ankle playing basketball in my PE class at the end of the school year. When the summer started, I was in a cast and not able to move around very well. My mother saw that I was at a pivotal place in my life, and was well aware that my behaviors would not encourage me to stay on a straight path with the many temptations I would be facing in high school.

She made a decision to send me to the same drug ministry my dad attended that had allowed him to get his life in order. I wasn't an addict, but she knew that me being surrounded by people who had severely damaged their lives based on their choices would help me. The experience did just that. One guy at the facility took me under his wing. He had just been shot up pretty bad, to the point he was still nursing some of his gunshot wounds. He took his time to let me know that I was headed down the wrong path with the people I was choosing to hang around. He really wanted me to see my life in his and not end up where he did. He took me around the facility every day and introduced me to people, and they motivated me, through their stories, to clean up my life. There were some amazing stories. One guy had survived gunshots to his head and took my finger and placed it on one of the bullets still lodged under the skin.

I don't know if my mother knows this, but this was a turning point in my life. After a week or so, my mother came to my rescue and allowed me to go home. My perception of the world around me changed for the better, as I saw where my life was headed if I didn't create a different vision for my life.

Shortly after returning home from my visit to the drug rehabilitation facility, I celebrated my fourteenth birthday. My parents bought me a basketball goal that I could play on outdoors. My dad and I assembled it together, and it became my day-and-night passion. If you came past my house, you had to play me no matter who you were. I still had my cast on, but it didn't keep me from playing from sunup to sundown every day.

Create a New Vision

Not only did I have the drive to be a great basketball player, I also had the height that could likely make my basketball dreams a reality. Before I broke my ankle, I just played basketball with no sense of purpose or awareness of where the game could take me. People marveled at my height, to be only fourteen years old and legitimately six feet three inches tall. The voices of people at the drug facility telling me not to waste my God-given talents echoed through my mind with every jump shot I took on my new basketball court.

The summer before I entered high school, it just all made sense: I had the ability to make something of myself through the game of basketball. I no longer was just another tall, talented kid; I was now equipped with a vision. My life changed entirely for the better when I created a new vision for my life. It dawned on me that possibly my struggling mother wouldn't have to pay for my education if I was able to obtain a college basketball scholarship while playing in high school. My vision that summer was to obtain a basketball scholarship and obtain a free education in college.

When my vision changed, everything else that was not a part of my vision was naturally removed from my life. Suddenly, hanging out past my curfew, smoking weed, had no appeal to me. I found myself out of town on a regular basis with my AAU basketball team, playing against some of the best fourteen-year-olds in the country. The pursuit of my vision created a new set of friends and a new reality. I entered high school a new man, in whom people could see a noticeable change. My vision was set. The classroom is what made sense to me, as I had to get good grades to stay eligible to play basketball. My friends changed to people who had the same vision as me, which helped us to keep each other focused. My vision rearranged my entire life for the better.

Creating a vision for your life gives you the same power to change as you saw in my story. You may not have the skill or dreams to become a great athlete, and that's okay. We all have gifts in life that we can create a vision of success by pursuing. Don't ignore your gifts and talents, no matter how young or old you are, because these are the things that bring a clear sense of purpose and allow you to excel in life.

Some of you may say to me, "Hey, I'm already on track and have not had the same struggles you experienced." I say to you: stay on the right track, and create an even larger vision for your life.

You Can Change Right Now!

No two life situations are exactly alike.

> *Wherever you are in life, you can create change for yourself in this exact moment by creating a different vision for your life.*

Wherever you want your life to go, create the vision inside of yourself and see yourself living in that vision. It may be hard to actually believe you can live in a completely different vision than where you are now, but if you picture it enough times in your mind, you will give yourself a fighting chance to live it.

You are not what the media says you are as a young black man. You are not what society says you are as a young black man. You are whatever the vision you create inside of yourself says you are.

A successful man always has a larger vision for his life than where he is.

What happens when you accomplish your vision? You create an even larger vision. After you accomplish that larger vision, then what do you do? You create an even larger vision. There is never an end to what is possible for your life if you always have a vision.

Embrace the Power of Vision

The power of vision is that no one can create it except for you. People can suggest things to you, and offer you guidance on how to live your life, but the power of vision is squarely in your hands, because no one can create your life's vision except for you. There is unlimited power and potential in creating a vision for your life. Have a conversation in your mind, and tell yourself that you are the only one responsible for creating change in your lifetime. See the change you would like to experience, and then embrace the power of the vision by taking the necessary steps to live it.

Create a larger vision for your life, and do it *now*!

Notes and Insights

Notes and Insights

Chapter 2: Create Your Own Reality

Being a young black man of twenty-eight years, I have experienced some things that have made me very aware of the struggles young black men face on a daily basis in society. When I began driving luxury automobiles in my early twenties, it became almost commonplace to be stopped for no apparent reason. I can remember one time in particular when I was stopped for "not coming to a complete stop at a stop sign." The officer quickly asked me if I had large amounts of cash in my vehicle, which was a point-blank way of asking me if I was a drug dealer.

When the CNN special *Black in America* hit the airwaves, it was an attempt to let America know of the struggles black people face when they wake up every morning. There is one quote from the CNN series that summarizes the placement and treatment of black men in America: "An educated black male is the equivalent of an uneducated white male with a criminal record." This means that an uneducated white male with a criminal record has an equal chance to get ahead in society as a black male with a college degree. Please keep in mind that these statistics are from CNN, the most trusted news source in the world.

It doesn't end there when it comes to media portrayal of black men in America. Just look at the news and many shows, like *The First 48*, which airs on the A&E network and really should be re-titled *Blacks Killing Blacks.* This show follows detectives attempting to solve murders, of which most are young black males killing each other, across the various inner cities across America. I'm not implying that there is some design to the way young black men are depicted on the show, but if you watched it enough, it would naturally instill beliefs about young black men that might make you careful in the way you interact with them.

If you turn on the videos where black rappers talk of killing, drug dealing, and womanizing constantly, this can't help but instill beliefs that could translate in someone's mind as the reality of how young black men are. As a young black man, if you see these images I mention enough, it's not difficult to believe that this is the mold you are supposed to fit. The media has a huge influence on how we see ourselves as young black men. If you don't believe me, observe the styles that the rappers exhibit, and look around you at the styles of young black men who mirror these rappers and entertainers.

The reality that is imposed upon us as young black males is serious, creating a need in me to expose that we have the power to create a reality that is the opposite of what is constantly fed to us through our surroundings. I suggest creating your own images of success through looking at black men who have made significant contributions by going in the opposite direction of what the media and society says we are. Although society paints a clear picture of what they think we are as young black men, the truth is that many of us have "made it." We have a young black man by the name of

Barack Obama who occupies the most coveted position in America: president of the United States.

Growing up in elementary school, I remember reading Dr. Ben Carson's book *Gifted Hands* cover to cover. His words gave me a clear picture of what was possible for my life as a young black man, as I saw the struggles he faced in a single-parent household to how he made it as a world-renowned surgeon who was the first to successfully separate Siamese twins. His success created a different mental image of what was possible for me. I am encouraging you to do the same: find the black men who have accomplished things you wish to accomplish with your life, and allow that to erase the negative images that are imposed upon us as young black males and replace them with positive images of success. After all, it is possible, and this message becomes stained on your mind the more images of possibility you take in.

The Power of Self-Development

The power of self-development is vital in the young black man positioning himself to succeed in life. What is meant by self-development is seeking out messages of people who specialize in helping others get to where they want to be in life. These types of messages come from people like me who are motivational speakers. They may also come from a pastor or minister of a church. Underneath it all, the messages you digest the most will dominate the way you think and form your outlook of the world around you.

Ultimately, the messages you take in, as well as the images you take in, will control what kind of reality you will paint for your life.

Reality in this instance means how big of a picture and vision you are willing to create for your life, based on how much you believe in yourself.

These words are birthed from personal experiences. I tell you, with every ounce of belief I possess, that self-development works. It is responsible for every remarkable accomplishment I have achieved in my life. Self-development created a story in my mind that nothing was beyond my reach. It is my desire that this same story begins to formulate in your mind with every turn of the page.

When I was twenty-two years old in my last semester of college, I decided that I was going to be a motivational speaker. For someone that age to choose this occupation coming right out of college is basically unheard of. This is a profession traditionally reserved for older people who have had some sort of life-changing event that makes people find inspiration in their story. I didn't fit that mold, but I believed I had a gift that could help people find their way in life. Sometimes when you are young and have high aspirations in life, people will look at your youth as a handicap.

By all means, disregard negative opinions about your dreams, and test the waters of what's possible for your life.

Days after I graduated from college, I began writing my first book, *The Universe is Inviting You In*. It was a battle, in that many people didn't take me seriously because of my age and looked at my ambitions to become an author as being premature. Although I had a college degree, I didn't immediately go for a high-paying job like many of my college classmates. I chose to pursue my dream of becoming an author and motivational speaker instead.

In the beginning of writing my book, I shared my aspirations with people I looked up to, most notably my pastor and his wife. They encouraged people in the congregation to update them via fax about what was going on with their lives. One day after church, my pastor's wife pulled me to the side and said, "What makes you think you can write a book? We haven't even done that yet!" I was paralyzed in that moment because I thought I would receive encouragement for following my dreams and doing something that could change the direction of people's lives for the better.

That event didn't deter me one bit. It simply made me smarter knowing that, in life, not everyone will see your dreams as clearly as you do. Even though this is true, and you will encounter opposition when attempting to live your dreams, that's never a reason to stop! I embraced the power of self-development even more after that and listened to one of my favorite motivational speakers, Dr. Wayne Dyer, every morning as I woke up. What this did was create a story in my mind that nothing was impossible as I aspired to finish my first book.

Sometimes you just have to put your head down and complete your tasks in life. I don't mean put your head down in shame, rather to not be distracted and remain focused as you do what's necessary to live your dreams. Before I knew it, my book was complete. I then had a mind-blowing idea that many would view as impossible. I wanted to get the top black motivational speaker in the world, Les Brown, to write an endorsement for my book. It was a long shot, but I figured why not go for it?

I went on Les Brown's website to see his speaking schedule, only to find he would be in my hometown of Prince George's County,

Maryland, in the coming weeks. I sent a raw, unedited version of my book to a store to have copies made to give to him. When Mr. Brown came to town, I was right there to hear him speak. After he finished, he was mobbed by all of his adoring fans, and I waited for an opening to talk with him. This opening presented itself, and I boldly presented my book to him and his staff and asked if they would write an endorsement if they liked it.

One month went by, and it was time for my book to be printed. I had completed the entire publishing process, but had not heard back from Les Brown, so I figured I had given it a shot and his endorsement just wasn't going to happen. The day my book was scheduled to go through the printing press, the final step in publishing a book, I received an e-mail from Les Brown's staff saying they loved my book. What also accompanied this e-mail was this testimonial from Les Brown himself:

> *The Universe Is Inviting You In* is a great tool on the road to your destiny. Each of us must choose our path and utilize the knowledge and wisdom that is guiding our journey from within, giving us the power to live our dreams. –Les Brown, "The Motivator"

The Power of Opinions

A person's opinion of what they believe is possible for your life has no power unless you allow it to. Imagine if I had accepted the opinion that I was too young to write my book and "what makes you think you can do this…?" If I would have accepted those opinions, I likely would have given up and not experienced the success that has kept me on a path to write this book to enhance your life for the better. The above story ends with my first book selling thousands of copies worldwide, with countless people telling me how much of a blessing my words have been to their life. This is not to brag in any way, but the reality of what would have happened if I had allowed a negative opinion to dictate my belief in myself is too evident to ignore.

Self-development is the ultimate defense mechanism against any words you encounter that don't encourage you to live your dreams. Self-development is for the dreamer, the person who is not satisfied with being average in this average world.

> *The world's system programs you to be average and to just exist and get by; self-development reprograms your mind to go after everything that is uncommon, to not be afraid to test the boundaries of life.*

Never take a negative opinion personally. The energy it takes to address a negative opinion is energy that could have been spent working on your dream or expanding your vision of possibilities for your life. In reality, when that person went out of her way to discourage me from living my dreams, it came from a place that she couldn't see herself doing what I aspired to do with my life.

> *Many times people will discourage you from living your dreams because they can't see themselves doing the things you see yourself doing in life.*

In essence, they view you through the lens of what they believe is possible for their own lives. Plenty of negative opinions that will come your way when you attempt to break the norm of society are based in a person's own insecurities.

> *Don't engage in conflict with negative people. Just pivot and move forward.*

Ironically, the same people who doubted me while I was writing my book actually came to me for help and advice after I published it. I kept a good heart and helped them to get their dreams out. When your heart turns bad, usually everything you attempt to produce and create goes sour. It's important to not hold grudges while pursuing your dreams. If someone doesn't see eye to eye with you, just keep moving in silence. They'll respect your rise to the top when it's all said and done. Don't be an "I told you so" person when you make it in life. Stay humble, as staying grounded allows you to focus on the next, greater task that awaits us all.

You have the power to shape your own reality. Never accept a reality that doesn't line up with where you see yourself going in life. Seek out images and messages of possibility until this is your normal way of thinking. Never stop engaging in self-development. The greater the message of possibility rings in your heart and mind, the larger vision you will establish, and the higher you will go in life. Be you.

Notes and Insights

Notes and Insights

Chapter 3: The Power of Appearance

We live in a society where opinions about you are formed based on your overall appearance, before you say one word out of your mouth. The most constant images we see of ourselves as young black men in the media are with our pants sagging, engaging in some sort of mischief, while going nowhere fast. This does not have to be you. You do not have to appear as the rapper does, with your pants hanging low, with every other phrase being "you know what I'm saying."

Always strive to look your best. When I suggested that you focus on images of black men who have made something of themselves in life, you'll observe that they wear successful attire. Not clothes hanging low, with bandannas, but rather nice suits and clothing that reflects they are going somewhere in life. I don't have to get too specific. We all know the message that certain attire suggests as to the type of people we are.

Society expects a certain look from young black men. Surprise people when they see you. When I decided I was going to be a motivational speaker, one of the first things I did was notice how they dressed. When I was being trained, one of the trainers said, "You're never off as a speaker." He meant people expect a certain image of success when they see you, because of your message and who you are. That message is not specific to me because I'm a motivational speaker; it's specific to us all as young black men if we would like to project an image of success.

You may not have made it to where you want be in life yet in terms of achieving your vision, but that doesn't mean you can't look the part. Human beings are programmed to judge you based on what they see. I'm not saying this is right in any way. In reality, it's just the way it is. When you have the look of where you want to be in life, you take on the spirit of that thing even though you haven't arrived yet. Every time I saw legendary motivational speaker Les Brown, he had on a nice tailor-made suit, with a perfectly groomed appearance. I knew I wasn't as good a speaker as he when I first started, but I was smart enough to adopt his image. In doing this, my appearance commanded a respect from people that made them want to hear what I had to say.

Be A Person of Power

There is power in your appearance. To be the powerful young man that you are, it needs to be reflected in your dress. Even if you can't afford the nicest clothing, take pride in how your clothes look. Keep them clean and ironed. This will command respect and suggest that you have a high level in which you carry yourself. Do away with the "I just rolled out of bed" look. Clothes that have been cared for suggest that you operate on a successful level in all that you do.

Stay groomed and manicured. A young black man should always have a pair of hair trimmers to make sure his appearance is always tight. Your grooming habits should never slip, as you want to come across with a level of excellence in all you do. Stay trimmed up in between barber visits, and be consistent. People admire and respect consistency in our society. This trait is something that many people lack. Consistency reflects good habits and dedication. You never know who is watching you from afar. There can be someone watching you who you are not aware of who is holding the key to your next big opportunity in life.

Adopting these habits ensures that the first impression you make on anyone will be excellent. You get only one chance to make a first impression. Be a role model to other young black men around you. We know the images we see of ourselves on a daily basis in society. I'm not saying they are all bad, but the majority of images we see of ourselves in media outlets are not images that portray success. My older sister always told me to reach out to the youth when I became a speaker. She said, "You have no idea how just seeing a black man in a suit could impact a young man for the better."

This was so true. Many young black men very seldom see a black man who has a successful appearance. To you, young black man: make the choice to carve out a space of success for yourself through a powerful appearance.

Conversations for Success

I'll never forget being on a date with one of the most beautiful young women I had ever laid eyes on. I was twenty-four years old. She was so enamored with the fact that I didn't have to curse every other word and, in her words, that I wasn't "talking about stuff like Lil Wayne." When she said these words to me with a huge smile on her face, I said to myself, *Is this what guys really talk to this beautiful young woman about on dates?*

A young man who is articulate and uses words that aren't in line with the latest slang has appeal not just to women, but people in general. Reading is an excellent way to expand your vocabulary. Society is hungry for young black men who have a powerful appearance, who articulate their words, who are not afraid to break the mold of what the media says we are. Take a good look at your president, Barack Obama. He has paved the way for society to accept the articulate young black man. During his presidential run for office, the world fell in love with this well-manicured, good-looking, articulate black man. That same world is waiting to fall in love with you, and is more open than ever to the possibility of what you have to offer.

I will never forget the change in white people's perception of me when I would do book signings at a very prominent venue in Washington, DC, on the weekends. I had frequently been at this venue in the prestigious Capitol Hill area of DC for years, and I could count on one hand how many white people had actually purchased my books. During President Obama's presidential run, all of sudden, they wanted to hear what I had to say and, above all, were open to my message. It wasn't me; it was the climate that our president set with his powerful appearance, which has opened more doors than ever for us as young black men. Your time is ***now***! The shift has taken place. The questions remain: Will you shift with the climate? Will you adopt a clean-cut and manicured appearance? Will your attire say to someone that you are headed somewhere in life? This is the choice I set before you my young black brother.

The Eye-to-Eye Stance

Look people in the eye when you speak to them. It conveys confidence. People are attracted to confidence, and oftentimes follow those who are confident. With your appearance intact, with eloquent speech, it's confidence that will complete you. You have nothing to be ashamed of as a young black man, so look up! When you meet people, confidently introduce yourself with a firm handshake and be sure to look them in the eye. Love yourself, young black man, and be sure of yourself.

> *Confidence is an intriguing trait that makes people want to know more about you.*

People will deal with you if they can perceive a true confidence coming from you. This is an attractive trait because many people lack overall confidence in life. It is an attractive trait because if a person cannot find confidence within themselves, they'll want to be around you, as they can find a sense of confidence in you. Confidence opens up many doors in life.

Attract the Woman You Want

A solid woman who is educated and focused in life wants a man with the same attributes. There is such a shortage of black men out there that many women have been forced to lower their standards when going down the list of what they want in a man. If your appearance and drive in life are intact, it can overwhelm them in a good way. Believe me, women will easily let go of something that is not up to their standards when they meet a man who fits their mold.

This starts through the first conversation. This conversation cannot take place if your appearance does not match the mold of what she wants. The real conversations in life are the ones that don't verbally take place. A woman is looking at your appearance while you are using whatever line you use to attract her, and her decision to continue interaction with you is based mainly on your initial appearance.

If a woman is on the right track in life and you approach her with a street type of look, with your pants sagging, all she will see is the continuation of the death cycle of young black men that you represent, and she will want no part of you. A solid woman is not looking for the gangster and thug type. She is hopeful that maybe, just maybe, she will find a solid man with ambition and drive. Be that man for her. Allow your well-manicured and well-spoken appearance to have a conversation with her that is unspoken. When women pass you by, let your appearance provide hope that we are not all lost as young black men, and that the good ones are not extinct. Does your appearance tell her that you are worth a conversation to get to know her?

The Power of a Level

This chapter really isn't about appearance itself, rather the level that your appearance tells people you are on. It is important to establish a vision for your life, and understand the level you must be on to fulfill your vision. If you don't have a vision in life, there is no need to think about the importance of appearance and the message it sends to people about your level. A person who has a vision of success shows it through his overall demeanor. A certain level is communicated with people they come in contact with. When it comes to this type of person, you will hear phrases like "That person is sharp."

Understand that with a vision comes the need for you to appeal to people who can help you get there. I have never seen anyone zapped to a destination in life before. What I have seen repeatedly is people being assisted by other people to get to where they want to be. People want to be able to trust you. Your appearance weighs heavily on whether they will even start the conversation that determines if they can benefit you.

You don't want to be the person who is full of gifts, talents, ideas, and genius, but they are covered up by the wrong appearance.

Understand the importance of what your up-front look communicates to people in terms of where you are going in life. Realize that whether or not you think it is fair, rules exist in society regarding appearance.

Play the game to win, and respect the fact that your up-front game determines whether any conversation is furthered.

Notes and Insights

Notes and Insights

Chapter 4: The Power of Education

Education is one of the most powerful tools at our disposal as young black men. With the dropout rates being at an all-time high amongst our youth, the value of education is deteriorating in the minds of not just young black men, but youth as a whole. It's very difficult to get ahead without an education. We live in the era of one of the most serious depressions to have taken place in decades.

A recession is when unemployment is higher than usual as a result of less opportunity being available to everyone as a whole. Recessions make job hunting very competitive. If you are not at least a college graduate, then securing a well-paying job is something you will find very difficult. I have heard countless stories of how the recession has affected many families who were actually doing great financially. I have seen the effects of the recession on my own family, with relatives who were once making large amounts of money suddenly at the mercy of their reversal of fortune, and scrambling just to get by.

Education is Nonnegotiable

What I mean by nonnegotiable is that it is not even worth thinking about getting ahead in life without an education. It's too difficult, with us living in the most competitive era in history. The recession is so real that people with master's degrees and PhDs are struggling to find work. I have personally seen five of my close friends all lose their jobs in the last two years, through no fault of their own. Companies just no longer had the funds to pay them and had to eliminate jobs just to keep the company from financial ruin.

With a climate existing where even educated people are struggling, where do you think that leaves the uneducated? That leaves them hanging on for dear life, taking jobs that pay next to nothing, with struggle as their fate. Hopefully I have painted a picture of what it is like to be uneducated in this society.

I learned in my Psychology of Crime class in college that the number one cause of crime is status frustration. What this means is that people who aren't doing well get tired of looking at people who are doing well and get frustrated. This frustration leads to people saying, "I'm going to get ahead by any means." "Any means" oftentimes leads to illegal activity. At the root of it all are people unwilling to get an education so they can get a well-paying job to attain the things they want from life.

Don't get me wrong, some people who do not go to college still figure out a way to get ahead. Some people may take up a trade, like barbering, electrical work, or plumbing. But underneath those trades, they still had to get an education in order to effectively do those jobs.

There were others I observed after I graduated from college who turned to the streets, many of whom began dying as a result of their street life of crime. It was amazing how the people I least expected turned to crime after high school. I don't genuinely believe they wanted to live that life, but saw it as the only way to accumulate the things that educated people had from working their jobs and being smart with their money. I urge you to not get caught in that trap. Do well in school, and find a way to further your education after high school.

What you value in life becomes evident in the results you get with your own. If you value education, then the fruits of your values will ultimately lead to a college degree. If fun is more important than education, then you'll find yourself looking up at people who valued an education, wondering what happened to you. You're young, so naturally, fun is a high priority. With this being said, as you mature, your values should adjust to where you begin to look beyond where you currently are in life, and see the bigger picture of where you want to be.

The power of vision is stressed repeatedly because this is your life-preserver that will keep you afloat no matter what you face. I'm urging you to create a vision for your life, no matter where you are, and see yourself as arriving at the end you have in mind. When you look at the end of where you want to be, and observe the reality of what it takes to get there, you will see that education is a main factor for you to achieve your vision in life. Have your fun—hang out on the weekends; go to your football and basketball games—but buckle down when it comes time to succeed academically.

Comeback Power

Honestly, I had my struggles academically in high school and college. There was one instance, after my sophomore year in college, that my grades were so bad I was facing academic probation. I worked hard; I just had a difficult time keeping up with the material.

I came home for the summer and talked with my parents about it, and my dad said, "Well, you know what you have to do. You have to man up!" He was saying that I had to do what it took to come back strong from my situation. I then went back to school my junior year and began making 3.00 grade averages, which would progress to 3.50 grade point averages for the better part of my upperclassman years in college.

You may be in a place where you feel as though you can't make a comeback academically, but I beg to differ. It's just a matter of focusing on the solution to your academic problems and not the problem itself. When you focus on the problem, it becomes the only thing you think about in your mind. When problems dominate your mind, it's difficult for you to entertain a solution to them. I am respectfully asking you to "man up" and do what it takes to create the academic outcome you wish to experience if you aren't where you want to be. If you are where you want to be, I challenge you to create a larger vision and work hard to achieve even greater success. This is the mind-set of a champion.

In my sophomore year of high school, I faced the very dilemma I just discussed concerning my grades. I was in the middle of the year, and I just couldn't seem to get my grades together. I was on the verge of not getting a 2.0 and sitting out the remainder of my basketball season. This was a critical time for me because my vision and dream was to play basketball in college on a full athletic scholarship at a Division I school. I had to miss a couple of games in the middle of the season to ensure that my grades were satisfactory enough to continue to play basketball. In life, you may have to take a step back in order to take a leap forward.

I did what I had to do and got a 2.0 that quarter. I was eligible to play, but knew that a 2.0 was far from where I needed to be if I was going to attract college coaches to recruit me.

Athletic aspirations are nothing without academic aspirations.

Eventually, in my senior year of college, I did land the Division I college scholarship I dreamed of, but it wasn't strictly because of my athleticism and jump shot. When my college coach called to let me know that I was being offered a full athletic scholarship, he spoke equally of my academic performance as he did my athletic performance. He said, "I was impressed by how you turned your grades around after your sophomore year. That says a lot about you."

In a sense, my academics were a deal sealer. They can be a deal breaker for you as well. My junior year and beyond in high school, I maintained a 3.0-plus GPA. It's not necessarily how you begin. Your value in life is determined by how you finish.

Seeing your academic performance as a potential deal maker is a great outlook to have. You could be competing for a job after college, and guess what employers do: They review your academic transcripts. They see your ability to handle your college course work as a clue to what kind of worker you will be. The fact that you graduate from college is not good enough in some instances; sometimes it's your performance in college that will determine whether you get the job you want. Above all, see value in education no matter where you are. It's never too late to create a new beginning for yourself in life. This could be academically or in anything else you aspire to do in life. Knowledge is the key to your best life possible.

Education Outside of the Lines

When speaking of the power of education, I purposefully spoke of a traditional academic education first, as without question, it will help to create the life you want live as an adult. There are other forms of education in life that take place outside of the classroom. People pay you for what you know and how effectively you do a certain thing. Look at the NBA. You can go check the players' salaries and see the players who perform better get paid significantly more than players who perform averagely.

A player's performance gets better as he works on his game and improves his weaknesses in the off-season. If you come into the NBA and are a solid player, but cannot shoot the ball, it is your job as a professional to improve that aspect of your game in the off-season. The player who comes back as an improved shooter has permission from the coach to shoot the ball more. That player usually ends up scoring more points, and when his contract is up with a team, and that player has shown improvement during their first contract, then the team has to pay him more money to keep him. If a player has a weakness in his game that he doesn't work hard to fix, then usually that player is traded or released from that team. If you have ever seen a young player who was in the NBA, but suddenly wasn't there anymore, chances are he had a weakness in his game that wasn't fixed. He didn't seek the education it would have taken to improve the weakness, and he suffered financially for it by no longer having a job in the NBA.

As a motivational speaker, I knew the importance of being educated before I went out and began my speaking career. I sought education from some of the best speakers to give me an understanding of the speaking industry. As my understanding increased as a result of nontraditional classroom education, my effectiveness as a speaker improved, resulting in more personal success in my business.

Even now, being in the industry for six years, I still attend classes to increase my knowledge on the changing trends in the speaking industry. This knowledge creates more value, because I now train other speakers as a result of the knowledge I have accumulated. Knowledge is value. This value creates a more effective and successful you.

You must do whatever it takes to get a high understanding of what you aspire to do in life. Many college students further their education of the field they want to enter during their summer breaks by interning at companies. Interning is nontraditional education, but it creates a high level of understanding of the field they aspire to enter. Sometimes I would go watch other speakers just to pick up on things and educate myself. I would see how speakers sold their products from the stage without the audience even knowing.

When you get in the atmosphere of where you want to be, everything around you becomes alive, and a higher level of understanding is inevitable.

Think outside of the lines in terms of getting education. Some of the most potent forms of understanding take place outside of the classroom. Every aspiration has creative ways of learning about it. Ask yourself: what can I do to create a higher understanding of the place I want to be in life? Listen to the answer inside of yourself, and don't be afraid to venture out. Life is not always lived in straight lines. Value education and the many forms it comes in.

Notes and Insights

Notes and Insights

Chapter 5: The Power of Audacity

The entrance to your life's ambition is through a door called "audacity." Audacity is the much bigger brother of confidence.

> *Audacity is confidence in action, and it is the epitome of going after what you want in life with no fear of what you will encounter along the way.*

If you want the quintessential picture of audacity, it is in a house at 1600 Pennsylvania Avenue Northwest, Washington, DC. Friends, this is the address to the White House, which houses the most audacious man in history, a man I am proud to call my president.

Think of the audacity it took to run for the most elite office this world has to offer, the US president, in a world where an educated black man is the equivalent of an uneducated white male with a criminal record. There have been many predecessors to President Barack Obama, such as Martin Luther King Jr. and Malcom X. These men of audacious nature weren't afraid to blaze trails for black people in conditions of racial injustice that made many black men say, "Why even try to escape the injustices of segregation?" The spirit of audacity in these innovators was greater than any realities that surrounded what they believed was right, with nothing but death keeping them from the fight for equality and justice for blacks.

Leaders possess confidence; innovators possess audacity. People will naturally follow a confident leader, because confidence is a very intriguing trait that draws people in. People will become a part of the movement of an innovator; an innovator is beyond a confident person because they are attempting to do something that has never been done. People want to be a part of such movements, as we witnessed in the 2008 presidential campaign of Barack Obama. As crazy as it seemed for a black man to become president of the United States, as then Senator Barack Obama gained momentum in the polls, more people hopped on board in support of him. He did represent a change this country drastically needed, but his audacity captivated people who could do nothing more than believe it was possible for him to win.

Your vision in life is fueled not just by belief, but also the audacity to go after it. President Barack Obama wrote a book titled *The Audacity of Hope*. A title like this suggests if you are to accomplish anything significant in life, audacity must be present to fuel the hope that sees past all obstacles.

I submit to you today that as a young black man, confidence is not enough en route to your life's destination. Your power is in your audacity to remain confident in spite of the many ups and downs you will face.

Let Me Further Paint this Picture

In my junior year of high school, I was a starter on the boys varsity team. I didn't achieve the statistical success people had hoped I would during that season, scoring no more than six points a game. These are not statistics that entice Division I college basketball coaches to recruit a player. Nonetheless, audacity was all I had at the end of my senior season to believe I could still obtain a Division I basketball scholarship.

I didn't feel I received a fair shake my junior season and respectfully informed the coaching staff I would pursue my basketball endeavors at a different school for my senior season. Deep down, my coach understood my decision, although it was not something he was happy about. I remember being in the gym after school with him soon after I informed him I was leaving. We were talking in front of some of my teammates, of which one was a senior with no scholarship offers on the table. We were discussing my reasoning for leaving, and I expressed that I wanted to give myself a chance to play Division I basketball.

My teammate then said, "You're not built to play Division I basketball."

My coach then indirectly corrected him and said, "He can play. He has a real shot." I respected my coach for that. He could have taken a cheap shot at me because I was leaving his basketball program, but he told the truth that everyone knew.

My mother discouraged me from making the move to another school for my senior season with reasoning like: "You've been in school with your classmates for three years now. Why would you just up and leave your senior year?"

Audacity is being unafraid to make the hard decisions life presents us all.

Average people evade the truth that is staring them in the face. Great people stare at the truth and make clear decisions.

Audacity is being unafraid to "man up" and do what's needed to achieve any vision. I would say I was at a crossroads, but not leaving that school and staying in a situation that clearly was going to leave me stranded was a thought I never entertained. I was leaving no matter what anyone had to say.

Never be afraid to make decisions that make little sense to those around you when it comes to your dreams. Other people are never meant to share your clarity of where you want your life to go. A dream pursuit is something that must be done without apology! I transferred to a school that had wanted me for a while. I almost left at the beginning of my junior year, but I figured I'd let the season play out. After my junior season played out, the small voice within told me my time was up.

The new school I played at had a traveling AAU team that traveled all over the East Coast playing in tournaments to get our team exposure. The first tournament I played in was a huge AAU tournament in Philadelphia, Pennsylvania. As soon as I got out of the van we had traveled there in, I saw John Chaney, who was the head coach at Temple University. I then saw Steve Wojciechowski, who was an assistant coach at Duke University. I knew right then and there that I had made the right decision. Not only was I playing in front of Division I coaches, I was playing in front of some of the most recognized college coaches in America.

During the tournament, my shooting skills were on full display, and landed me many recruiting letters from Division I schools. When you have a vision, understand that you must place yourself in an atmosphere where your vision can become your reality. The more we traveled that summer, the more the recruiting letters poured in.

Finally, the school year started at my new school, and the student body was happy to have me as an addition to the basketball team. The first game of my senior season occurred, and it felt like the entire school was in the gym that night. There was a coach from Coastal Carolina University in the stands, scouting the game, looking for players to possibly sign to scholarships. I happened to catch his eye that night, which I didn't know until my new coach called me into his office and handed me a handwritten letter from the coach of Coastal Carolina University, expressing an interest in me and letting me know he would be recruiting me throughout the remainder of the season.

As my senior season progressed, my performance was the polar opposite of my junior season. I would regularly make the paper with my performances. Scoring twenty points in a game became the norm. My senior season was a complete turnaround, with many college coaches interested in signing me.

After the season, usually seniors have already signed a letter of intent to whatever college they want to play for. This was not my case. Coastal Carolina was the only Division I school showing any real interest in me. I had a handful of Division II schools I had visited, but my heart was set on going to a Division I school.

The signing period ends right before graduation and prom season, on May 15. Every day when I walked the hallways of my school, faculty and students alike would ask me if I had gotten signed yet. It was a little bit of pressure, but I still had hope I would go to the school where I wanted to go, Coastal Carolina University.

As the May 15 deadline approached for me to be signed, my high school coach sat me down in the same office he had handed me the letter from Coastal Carolina at the beginning of the season, looked me in the eye, and said, "Coastal Carolina is not going to sign you." He urged me to sign with one of the Division II schools that were offering me a partial scholarship. My mother, too, urged me to do the same thing, in the interest of her saving money on my education. This was a tough pill to swallow because at this point, I didn't see eye to eye with my coach or my mother about where I should go to college. I just had to go on my own island and stand with my decision to wait for Coastal Carolina to sign me.

With all odds stacked against me in terms of getting a Division I scholarship, I had one last trick up my sleeve. Audacity was giving me instructions, and I was listening. My accounting class was taking a field trip to tour the University of Maryland's campus. At the time, the University of Maryland Men's basketball team was ranked in the top ten of all of the colleges in America. I told my accounting teacher that I was going on the trip, but needed to step away at some point in time to go to the basketball office so I could talk with the coaches.

The day for the college tour came, and I went out there with a secret weapon: a game film to hand off to the coaches at the University of Maryland. I stayed on the tour for an hour or so before deciding to make my move. I stepped away from the group, with my game film in hand, and headed over to the athletic building. I found my way to an assistant coach of the basketball team. He immediately had a look of interest in his eyes when I introduced myself. At this time, I was six feet five inches tall, weighing two hundred pounds, with broad shoulders. I explained to him who I was and that I was a local basketball player from Prince George's County who had had an excellent senior season. I then gave him my game film and asked that he contact me if he was interested in having me come back to campus for a workout.

The assistant coach from Maryland contacted me two days later, saying he liked what he saw, and asked if I was available to work the summer camp to play with the players who were already there on scholarship. I was overjoyed because the University of Maryland men's basketball team had made it to the Final Four of the NCAA tournament. Coastal Carolina called me around May 15, as the signing deadline was approaching. I could tell they had their eye on other players ahead of me but were keeping in touch just in case one of them didn't want to sign with them. Coastal asked me what had been going on with me, and I told them that the University of Maryland was now actively recruiting me.

May 15 rolled around, and the only letter of intent I had in my living room was from a Division II school that really wanted me, but I just couldn't find it in my heart to sign with them. I tore the letter up and threw it in the trash. I was determined I was going to a Division I school, no matter what route I had to take to get there. On May 16, Coastal Carolina's head coach called to let me know they wanted to offer me a full athletic scholarship to play basketball for them. This was music to my ears, considering this was my dream. It was fulfilling to know that my audacity to wait for what I wanted ended in my being able to live my dreams.

In my story, from the time I transferred schools, to the time I received my basketball scholarship, there were countless instances in which I had to maintain a spirit of courage and audacity in the face of impossible odds. This story was not to brag or boast about my accomplishments, rather to paint a realistic picture of how audacity plays a huge role in accomplishing your dreams. Yes, the opposition was real, but the power of audacity proved to be greater than anything I faced. The end result says more than I ever could.

Be Realistic

There's a fine line between having audacity and purely living fantasies. I didn't write this book to give you confidence to become something you were never designed to be. Your vision should be created around your gifts and talents, the things you were born with that are clues to what you are supposed to be in life. Things don't just happen in life; they are the result of hard work and talent. I didn't just sit back and say I wanted to play Division I basketball. I did various things that benefited me in that quest. Audacity is being unafraid to set your dreams in motion, not sitting back waiting for magic to happen.

One of the best things I did was go on a visit to a Division I school my mother wanted me to visit for religious reasons. It was a Christian university that my mother thought would be good for me. I visited the school and did the whole tour thing, but I somehow found my way to the basketball office. The coaches took a look at my height and build and suggested I play with some of the players at open gym that day.

I met the players, and they welcomed me in. I had never played with a Division I college team before. This opportunity was a blessing because I was still in my senior year of high school. The pickup games began, and I held my own. The players were much bigger than what I was used to playing with, way stronger, and surprisingly more athletic. There were guys catching the ball and going up to dunk backward with an ease I had rarely witnessed in person.

This was good for my confidence because I knew I belonged on that level based on my performance. It was also good for me because it was a reality check and a wake-up call. I had a long way to go in spite of my size, talent, and scoring ability.

The reality was so startling of how big, strong, talented, and fast Division I basketball players were, that on the way back home from the university at 2:00 a.m., I asked my mother to drop me off at a twenty-four-hour basketball gym called Run-N-Shoot so I could immediately begin working on my weaknesses.

Fantasy or Reality

Even though you have the courage to go after what you want from life, some things may not always be for you. We are blessed with particular talents when we are born. As we get older, these talents become more evident. I am encouraging you to create a vision based on your natural talents. I stepped on the court with those Division I players to get a reality check. The verdict was that I wasn't living fantasies and I truly belonged on that level.

If you believe you belong on a particular level in life, go to where people are already freely operating on that level. Be honest with yourself when assessing whether you truly belong or not.

If you are in tune with reality, then you are not easily tempted to live fantasies. Don't be upset if you don't get some things from life that you really want. Life has the things waiting for us that are truly for us. If your vision was a little off, don't be afraid to create a new beginning that is centered in the reality of your gifts and talents. You cannot become just anything you want to be, but I promise you that you can become everything you are designed to be. Believe.

Notes and Insights

Notes and Insights

Chapter 6: The Entrepreneur in You

Opportunities are not always easy to come by in life, even when you do what is required to get them. This chapter is written in the spirit of creating your own opportunities, not waiting for them.

Being an entrepreneur is something my father instilled in me at a very young age. He didn't give me much growing up as far as material things, but he set me up for life by showing me how to create income for myself and, above all, create my own opportunities. Growing up, I had a natural hustler's instinct. In my early elementary years, I would buy football cards and sell the valuable ones to my classmates for a profit. In sixth grade, I was the candy man. I would go to the dollar store and buy candy and come to school and sell it for a profit.

My father was also pivotal in my operation. He worked at a warehouse where he could buy my candy at a wholesale price. He would bring home a box of one hundred Blow Pops, which I would have to pay him eight dollars for. I would then sell the entire box, and my net income would be twenty-five dollars. My gross income, which is the profit I made, would be seventeen dollars. Net income is the amount of money you generate from selling something. Your gross is the profit you make. Profit is the amount of money you make after you subtract your investment in whatever you sell.

It is profitable to understand the fundamentals of business and entrepreneurialism. An entrepreneur is someone who buys and sells goods, commodities, and services for a profit. No matter how old you are, you have the ability to become an entrepreneur. There are young entrepreneurs all around you. The kids selling cupcakes after church are entrepreneurs. The kids cutting grass in your community are entrepreneurs. The kids shoveling snow during the winter and raking leaves in the fall are entrepreneurs.

The key to being a good businessman and a successful entrepreneur is the ability to see a need and fill it. Another important characteristic of an entrepreneur is being fearless when it comes to creating opportunity for yourself.

Independence

Being an entrepreneur makes you independent. I can remember when I was in middle school and my dad brought me on board with his landscaping business. His client base was in the neighborhood he grew up in. Many of these people were elderly, and in need of someone to maintain their lawns for an affordable price. While my classmates were playing games and relaxing on the weekends, my father had me cutting grass and working in lawns with him.

I would come home from a good weekend of work and have a hundred dollars in my pocket. He paid me about ten dollars per yard. So if we cut ten lawns, then I would make a hundred dollars. As I got older, my dad gave me raises in acknowledgment of my hard work.

This allowed me to experience some financial freedom. I say "some" because I still depended on my parents for shelter, but I still was able to buy the latest Jordans and purchase the clothes I wanted. Never be afraid to work for what you want. You can begin living a financially independent life *now*! You're one idea or opportunity away!

The Recession

In the financial era we currently live in, a recession is well at work. A recession is when there are many people who are able to work, who have good qualifications, but are not working because of a shortage of job opportunities. It is important to begin thinking like an entrepreneur because the recession has been going on for years now, and no one really knows when it will end.

President Barack Obama recently addressed the recession at the end of 2011 in a town hall meeting. A town hall meeting is when a political figure talks to a concerned group of citizens in an intimate setting, and answers questions from members of the community. In this recent town hall meeting, many questions were asked of our president concerning the economy and where it is headed.

One of the president's answers directly stressed the importance of becoming an entrepreneur. He said, "American success is premised on individuals who have a great idea going out there and pursuing their dreams and making a whole lot of money in the process. That's great. It's part of what makes America so successful."

The president has to be careful about what he says in order not to offend people. I believe the president was saying, in this statement, that there is no end in sight for the recession we are currently facing. Your best bet is to go out there and create an opportunity for yourself. I interpreted his words to mean this because he spoke of how there are more people who are willing and able to work in America then there are jobs to fill. We have more able-bodied workers than jobs to be worked. This is the perfect storm that is responsible for what we are facing currently: a recession.

The Best Opportunities

The best opportunities are the ones that you create. I say this because you are in total control of an opportunity that you create for yourself. It goes as far as you will take it through dedication and hard work. Be sold on your ability to create opportunity, and create your opportunity with a sense of urgency. Urgency is important because many people who were doing very well financially at one time are now living in poverty because of the choice to rely on someone else for an opportunity.

Even if you have a job, you should always be creating an opportunity for yourself through exploring an entrepreneurial endeavor. You never know when a job could end, so having a backup plan that you created for yourself, is the perfect safety net. One question remains: what will you create?

See Yourself as an Entrepreneur

Even though you have the ability to become an entrepreneur, it becomes more real to you being around people who are living that life. If you have an idea, get around people who are already living it. If you do this, it is only a matter of time before you have the confidence to go after what you want in terms of becoming an entrepreneur.

Develop your mind as well. Entrepreneurship is not the traditional way to make a living in our society, so you may encounter resistance if you choose this route. It is important to have a strong mental barrier against any opposition that says you can't do it. In my earlier story of what I had to deal with when writing and publishing my first book, this statement comes alive. Listening to different motivational speakers and positive messages is what allowed me to be a successful entrepreneur and, ultimately, write these words to you today. When your mind is disciplined from you developing it, you will see opportunities other people seldom see. In turn, you will have success very few ever experience.

The last chapter was about education. My stance is still the same: educate yourself about what you aspire to do. The more educated you are about your craft as an entrepreneur, the more effective you will be, and ultimately the more money you will make.

Being courageous enough to become an entrepreneur is commendable, but you still need to be aware of the latest trends in your business to stay competitive. Education is free these days with the Internet being in place. You can find videos on practically anything on YouTube. You can Google search articles on anything as well. Be disciplined, and don't stop until you find the information you've been looking for.

Never stop educating yourself. Wealth finds its way to people who make education a lifelong experience.

Innovate

Being an innovator, as we discussed before, is being the first person to do something. Even if you don't know anyone who has done what you want to do, go after it! Have ambition and just do it. Some of the wealthiest people to have walked the earth are people who created what they saw within themselves and found the courage to go after what they wanted from life. You, too, possess this same ability.

Many of your black predecessors gave their lives so you could freely create what you want for yourself in yours. Pay tribute to them by not hesitating when it comes to your dreams.

It is my desire that you can see the possibility of becoming an entrepreneur as being real. Maybe you already were leaning toward becoming an entrepreneur before you read this chapter. Maybe you have a sudden idea that you would like to create. Either way, hold true to the fact that all we have is *now*. Do not wait to begin creating the opportunities inside of you. People who hesitate usually don't get what they want in life. People who are proactive, putting their ideas in motion and asking questions later, usually find themselves living above-average lives and accomplishing great things. Your power resides in the choice to create your life and do it your way.

Notes and Insights

Chapter 7: Guard Your Surroundings

One of my greatest realizations in life is that when I changed my surroundings, I changed. When my surroundings matched the vision I had for my life, the old me, who was headed nowhere fast, had no appeal. Your surroundings will dictate whether you live up to the potential you have in life. We are all created with gifts, talents, and abilities that make up our potential.

My potential flourished when I got around people and environments that catered to me growing as a young man and being my best in all I aspired to do. I believe your talents will shine bright when you surround yourself with the right people and environments for them to flourish. Every accomplishment I have mentioned in this book has come at the expense of me guarding my surroundings.

Surroundings are one of the most critical things we must create for ourselves in life. When I watch *The First 48* on A&E, it pains me to see young people going to jail for the rest of their lives because they didn't guard their surroundings. There was one episode, in particular, where a young man was asked to do a home invasion with two of his friends. The young man who put this plan together didn't really want to break into this man's house; he wanted to kill the owner of the house because the owner of the house had killed his father years ago, when he was just a young boy. He knew that if he could make it look like a home invasion that had gone wrong, instead of a cold-blooded murder, he would have a greater chance of getting away with the murder. He recruited two of his friends to help him, and told them they were just going to break into the house. The two friends had no idea what they were getting themselves into that night.

Shortly after the home invasion / murder took place, all three of the suspects fled on foot. One young man was apprehended just a few blocks away from the crime scene, out of breath. This was suspicious considering the police were aware of the home invasion / murder that had just taken place. When the police got the young man to the police station, they had him take his shoes off. The robbers/murderers had to kick the door in to break into the home. The police were able to see a very distinct shoe pattern on the murder victim's front door resulting from the force of the kick. As soon as the detective looked at the young man's shoe, he said, "We got you." His shoe pattern was an exact match to the one found on the door.

The detectives then asked the young man what had happened. He told a story that he was recruited to participate in a home-invasion robbery, and that his friend who recruited him told him they were just going to break into the house. He had no idea about his friend's plan to kill the owner of the house due to his longtime beef with the man.

Regardless of whether he was aware that a murder was going to take place, because he was there, he was charged with murder. All three of the gentlemen were apprehended and charged with murder. Many states have laws in place where everyone who plays a part in a crime is equally responsible, no matter what role they had. Two young men will sit in jail for the better part of the rest of their lives because they thought they were just going to do a home invasion. Above all, they didn't guard their surroundings.

Move Without Apology

When you create the type of surroundings that encourage you to be successful in life, you naturally will have to change your friends if they aren't the type of people who will help you to be your best. Sometimes these friends will try to criticize you because they know you are going on to bigger and better things. My advice is to let them say whatever they are going to say, but keep moving farther away from them and closer to your destiny.

It feels good when you know that you are elevating and doing better in life because you changed your surroundings. Only people who are like-minded and making progress in life should be allowed in your space if you want more from life than just being average.

Sometimes you can do everything right to people, but they still will hate you because you are doing better than them. This was one of the biggest adjustments I had to make as my books began to sell around the world and I began to get notoriety. I had friends who no longer wanted me around, as my success made them feel threatened. Whenever you gain success, never flaunt it in a way that makes people feel bad about themselves. Always stay humble. Just as fast as success comes, it can be taken away even quicker. Many people refer to this as a fall from grace. If you score twenty points in a game, or run for three touchdowns, be humble about it, and strive to be even better. When you get too full of yourself, usually you begin to think you are better than what you actually are, and people who work hard and stay their course will pass you by.

Keep in mind that, in most cases of success, some people you were on the same level with at some point will find a reason to bad-mouth you and bring your name down. When this begins to happen, be excited. This means you are actually making good progress in life and others are just jealous. Truthfully speaking, if people around you aren't turning on you, then I believe you aren't maximizing your potential.

When changing your surroundings, you can't worry about how people are going to feel. You are solely responsible for your success in life. You have the largest responsibility in positioning your life in a way that makes you a success. Guarding your surroundings is something that must be done without apology. People who worry about what effects creating a successful atmosphere will have on others will stay average.

> *Successful people make the hard decisions in life very few others are willing to make.*

You will offend some people on the way to the top. So be it.

Some people will talk behind your back, and others will confront you to your face, when you attempt to break the chains of average. I ask you to avoid conflict at all costs. When people talk about you, embrace the truth that people usually don't spend time talking about people who they think are average. Jealous people spend lots of time trying to make great people seem average in the minds of whoever will listen. Avoid conflict at all times. Your energy in your vision is what caused you to be great, so taking your energy to address people who talk negatively about you is a fast road back to average. Average people address everyone who they think wrongs them; great people simply choose to take the high road and stay the course toward their vision.

There is strength in people who aren't distracted by sideline voices. When you choose to live your vision and strive for greatness, view your life as a professional sporting event. Many people on the sidelines heckle and try to distract players during the game. The players hear them because they are human beings, but they choose not to acknowledge them because they are focused on the game. With all of your strength, stay focused on the game.

Show Me Your Friends...

"Show me your friends, and I will show you your future" is a powerful quote from author Mike Murdock. Essentially what he is saying is that people's lives usually go in the same direction of the people they spend the most time around.

In college, one of my professors discussed the groupthink mentality with us. He said that if you don't look, act, and live like the people around you, eventually you will be kicked out of the group. I didn't realize how true this was until I began to have major breakthroughs take place in my life that made it different from the people's around me, and their behavior toward me began to change.

If you desire a certain level in life, find people who are on that level, and get in their space. Usually you will be accepted because you all share similar interests. Their way of thinking will become your way of thinking, and you will all be positioned to achieve the common interest you share. It all comes back to vision and finding people who want the same things from life that you do. This way of thinking will ensure you have success in life.

You may be in a surrounding where it seems no one wants anything from life except to live day to day and do nothing. As a youth, it may be difficult to change your surroundings. You do have the power not to accept those kinds of surroundings. What I mean is that you can escape those surroundings mentally by aspiring to achieve more than what you see around you. I recommend reading books about the people you want to be like in life. These books provide a mental escape and create a picture in your mind of what's possible for you. If your mind can go to a place long enough, you will eventually follow.

Even if a way out of your surroundings seems impossible, if you focus on escaping those conditions, eventually a way out will reveal itself.

Maybe you want to be the first person in your family to graduate high school or attend college. Maybe you want to be the first person in your family to move out of a certain neighborhood. Whatever it is you envision for yourself, see yourself there until you actually are. Visualizing your success and working toward it in spite of any conditions is a formula for greatness. You have greatness within you.

If these concepts are hard to believe, then please use my life as an example. I grew up around drug addiction, and was in a single-parent household for the majority of my young life. No male that I knew of in my family had graduated from college. These were realities I had to deal with, but my power was in seeing myself beyond these realities and embracing the power to create my own.

I'm pleased to tell you that I graduated from college, have no drug addictions, and write books and speak to various audiences about how to be successful in life. When you hear of the realities I faced growing up, you wouldn't think this would be my fate in life. The bottom line is that it is. I am successful in spite of it all. There's another bottom line: you, too, can be successful no matter what you are facing in terms of your surroundings.

Average Versus Great

Average people make excuses as to why they cannot pursue greatness. Great people give themselves permission to be great no matter what challenges they face. Average people play the blame game in life, blaming other people for their shortcomings. Great people acknowledge all realities, but respect the reality to create their life, their way, according to their vision.

> *Average people whine and complain when they face life's adversities. Great people face adversity head-on and put their energy into creating a solution to life's inevitable problems.*

Read stories about great people, and you will find they all faced some sort of adversity to get to where they are in life.

> *As a young man, your transition into manhood is being able to stand tall in the face of adversity and finding a way to get up when life knocks you down.*

Part of the human experience is making mistakes and encountering adversity. Connecting with the greatness you possess depends on your ability to handle adversity. Your surroundings may be littered with unfavorable circumstances; you have the power as a young black man to find your way out, and into the place you see for yourself.

Greatness is You

I will end this chapter by proving that you have already accomplished greatness by simply being born. Let's observe the birth process. Only one sperm, out of four hundred million, makes it to the point that it can connect with an egg, creating an embryo. This embryo developed over the course of nine months, and you came into existence.

Let's examine the reality of how impossible this was: 399,999,999 of your brothers and sisters had to take a backseat to you so that you could arrive here and be born. You being here is proof that you have the power to overcome any surroundings, even if it seems impossible. You win a tremendous race with your unborn brothers and sisters to be born. If you won the race, it was intended for you to be great, or why else would you be allowed to win it?

There is a force above the world who knows all, who is responsible for you winning the race. This force gave you power to win many more races in your lifetime, even the ones of your youth. This force is well aware of your surroundings, but even more aware of the power you were born with to escape any unfavorable circumstances and achieve greatness.

If the reality of your environment ever overwhelms you, please remember: you won the race, and have the ability to cross any finish line.

Notes and Insights

Chapter 8: Respect

The ability to have respect for yourself and others will prove beneficial in life. Respect and a good attitude are personality traits that make you a desirable person to know and be around. When you give people respect in life, usually it is returned. Respect is the cornerstone of good relationships.

As a young black male, it is important to show respect to your authority figures. Authority figures have oftentimes seen a lot more than you as a youth, and have accumulated wisdom over the years. If you show them respect, they can easily guide you and help you make valuable decisions that will frame your life. Experience is a true teacher in life, and respect for your authority figures allows you to access the wisdom of their life experiences.

I believe many of our youth today are lost because of a lack of respect for anything. I see a tremendous amount of reckless behavior in our black youth that exhibits a lack of respect for everything around them, and ultimately for themselves.

We all need each other in life in order to get ahead. People will not always help you when you need help, but they are more likely to assist you when you approach them in a respectful manner. Respect makes you trustworthy. Being a respectful young man lets people know you have good self-discipline, and is reassuring in the fact that you know how to conduct yourself. Respect is a fundamental element we should all possess, but sadly, it is becoming less common with every passing day in our community.

Stand out amongst the crowd of young people by showing yourself respect, as well as others. This will open the many doors you need as you get older. The ability to show respect is something that is developed over time. If you do not know how to show respect to others as an adult, usually this behavior started as an adolescent.

How can you expect to be able to work for a living and provide for a family one day if you can't show respect? What happens if you get a job and don't show respect to your employer? You get fired.

Respect starts as a youth, when you are in school. It's important to stay in school because many of the attributes you will need to survive as an adult are developed there. If you can't respect your classmates, then usually you find yourself suspended from school. This is no different than being on a job and having to respect your fellow employees. Respect the ability to respect others as a building block of life.

Show Respect Even When It's Tough

In life, you will encounter people who you may not like. This will happen to us all, because as human beings, we naturally will not see eye to eye with everyone we interact with. With this being said, an important life skill is to continuously be able to show respect to people even if you don't like them. "Like" and "respect" are completely different things. You don't have to like everybody in life, but respecting everyone shows that you are a mature young man deserving of responsibility and opportunity.

It may be tough to respect people who don't have the same views as you. Maybe someone doesn't look like you, or they don't share the same religious beliefs. All the while, if you are going to succeed in life, you still have to respect these people.

Be Personable

Being personable is being easy to interact and communicate with. People like personable people. Personable people find a way to continue to succeed in life. Usually, well-liked, personable people make it to positions of leadership because people not only want to be around them, they have no problem following them. I am writing this book to help you become a leader in our society.

When you respect others regardless of how society perceives them, or what their beliefs are, it makes you relatable. When you see past a person's beliefs, or the stigmas society places on them, you can see the true person. People who can relate to various types of people by respecting them and not viewing them with prejudices are open to more opportunities in life. Think of the prejudices we have to overcome as young black men just for people of other races to respect us and take us seriously. We have amazing people in our race, and yes, success is prevalent in our race. With this being said, we are still fighting for respect as a race.

When you are tempted to look at someone as being less than you because they don't look or act like you, keep in mind the many prejudices we still face as young African American men, and freely give respect to all. Everyone deserves respect no matter what their past experiences were.

Be Considerate of Others

Being considerate of others doesn't make you a punk or a pushover. It is a decent thing when you cannot be considerate of just yourself and think of other people. It could be as simple as holding the door for someone behind you when you exit an establishment. It could be walking on the outside of the curb when you are on a date to protect the young lady you are with. You could help a sibling with his or her homework to be considerate. You could give your mother a compliment when she gets her hair done. Always think of ways to be considerate. Thoughtful, respectful people are a pleasure to be around.

Close Doors Gently

In life, relationships and interactions with people end. The way that interactions end is up to you. You have the choice to have them end in a disrespectful or respectful manner, even when you feel you've been wronged by someone. Having to have the last word and prove yourself at the end of a relationship often leads to an ugly split. Disrespectful phrases are usually said to someone in order to hurt them. In the example I am about to use, please see the benefit of closing doors gently.

I dated a girl briefly right after I graduated from college. I took her, out and we had an enjoyable time. We even hung out amongst friends after our first date. In one instance, she did something that I perceived to be very disrespectful and seemed a little off. I chose not to call her all kinds of names and disrespect her. I simply chose to end our interaction. When you are young and you are dating, this is commonplace for interactions to not last very long.

About three years later, I got an e-mail from this girl informing me that she knew someone who needed my business services. The opportunity was just what I was looking for at the time. I negotiated a fee and went on to do business with the person she referred me to, and made a large amount of money in the process.

Gently closed doors often lead to wide-open opportunities.

It takes a mature young man to see the bigger picture when your emotions can cause you to act in a disrespectful manner. Imagine if I would have disrespected this young lady? Do you think she would have led me to a well-paying opportunity?

There's a saying: "People don't remember you; they remember how you made them feel." Even when you disagree with someone, closing the door gently doesn't create an emotional explosion that could lead to people getting hurt. Be a smooth young man by avoiding conflict and gently ending interactions that you no longer wish to go on. You never know the opportunities you can create for yourself by closing doors gently.

A true leader is a leader because they don't get thrown off-balance when a conflict takes place. They see the best outcome, and their focus is not how to continue the conflict and win the battle; their focus is on an efficient solution to the problem so they can move forward toward things that really matter.

Average people will fight to the death to prove a point, even when an issue is dead and not worth fighting for. Great people are always looking for a solution and know how to manage a situation by maintaining an attitude of respect. Choose to respect people even when they don't respect you. This is the characteristic of a great leader.

How many times has our president been attacked for no apparent reason other than the color of his skin? There are people who say he is the most disrespected president in history. I very recently saw a woman who put her finger in the president's face. This man is the most powerful man in the world, holding the office of the president of the United States, and someone had the audacity to publicly disrespect him. His reaction was to simply walk away. Sometimes you just have to walk away. It doesn't make you less of a man to walk away from people who try to engage you in conflict. The president's reaction was one of strength. It had to be tempting to tell the woman, "Do you know who I am?" But just as he had done time after time before, he simply moved forward without engaging in conflict.

Remember that conflict requires two willing participants. If you are not willing, then there is no conflict.

Respect Yourself

A great way to practice self-respect is by putting yourself in situations to succeed. In the previous chapter, having respect for your surroundings was discussed, because respect for the surroundings you place yourself in is having respect for the potential that is inside of you. When you respect yourself, you can then easily respect others. I believe a large part of the many epidemics we see with young black males are due to a lack of respect for their own selves.

You have to respect yourself and the potential you have to succeed in life. Always place yourself in good situations for your potential to flourish.

Practice Safe Living

Life is a gift, and should be preserved at all costs through intelligent behavior. When you look good, you feel better about yourself. Find a sport, and play it on a regular basis. Childhood obesity is at an all-time high. This can be avoided by being active. When you aren't active, it leads to obesity and other health problems. Part of being successful is being healthy. How can you enjoy the success you've created for yourself if you aren't healthy? Exercise should be a habit. I am grateful for all of my years playing basketball, because they created healthy habits that have followed me into adulthood. You have the same opportunity to create good habits.

Be creative in the way you exercise. Make it fun by trying different things until you find what is most enjoyable for you. Maybe you're not into traditional sports. Try going for a jog with your favorite music playing in your headphones. See exercise as a necessity if you are going to live a healthy life.

Many of the bad health conditions we see in older people around us were set in motion in their youth through bad habits. Obesity doesn't just happen. It usually starts in youth and, if it's not controlled, continues into adulthood. Obesity puts strain on your organs and bone structure because they were never meant to handle all of the excess weight. This strain leads to many undesirable heath conditions that usually cut a person's life span short.

Maybe some of your exercising habits haven't been the best and you are already experiencing health problems in your youth because of it. Don't focus on what you did in the past; put your energy into developing a consistent exercise plan that will create a healthier lifestyle for you *now*.

Your diet also plays a huge role in how healthy you are. Try not to eat too much fast food. Many fast foods contain harmful chemicals that foods that you would cook at home don't have. Most fast-food menu items are also high in calories, which contribute to weight gain and unhealthy effects on your body.

Eat fruits and vegetables every day. These contain important nutrients that make sure you grow into a healthy young adult. They also give you more energy throughout the day and help you to learn and retain information better. A healthy diet can make you more productive each day, and allow you to perform better in the classroom.

Also, try to avoid junk foods like sodas, chips, and candy. Anything is okay in small quantities, but consuming too much junk food leaves you sluggish because of the low nutritional value. Taking in the proper types of nutrients is what you need to be a healthy young male.

Sexual Health

Ideally, I recommend that you abstain from sex until you are married, even in the midst of the vivid adult imagery that you can find on any television screen and in the lyrics of most popular music. The consequences of premarital sex manifest in various ways that can affect your physical health.

Many sexually transmitted diseases are alive and well in the world today. For the most part, they have no physical symptoms that can let someone know they if his or her partner has an STD. Most STDs are curable, while others result in death. The best way to avoid catching an STD, besides not having sex, is to have safe sex with a latex condom.

The young lady you are with may say something like, "I'm okay. I've gotten tested." Never take anyone's word for it. If you respect yourself, you will protect yourself!

One moment of pleasure could open you up to a world of health problems, not to mention death.

AIDS is an epidemic in our community. The United States Census Bureau states that African Americans make up about 13 percent of the United States population. That is a very low percentage. The Centers for Disease Control and Prevention, who has the job of tracking the progression of diseases, states that African Americans account for 46 percent of all HIV cases in the United States. HIV/AIDS is ravaging our community. Please protect yourself, or your life easily could be cut short from one bad decision.

If you choose to be sexually active, protect yourself and get tested for STDs on a regular basis, at least once every six months. If you have a partner, stress the importance of getting tested together and remaining monogamous with one another. In other words, don't cheat, because you open up to diseases not just yourself, but your partner as well. Respect yourself enough to care about your sexual health.

Recognize Your Value

If no one has ever told you this, you have value. You won the race and showed up here because something bigger than you knows how much value you really have. I believe in you. This is my reasoning for writing this book. I'm tired of our young black males conducting themselves in a way that does not command respect. When you value yourself, you respect yourself, because you are aware of your worth as a person. When you respect yourself, it is then very easy to respect others.

I don't care what the media says we are as young black men, portraying us as thugs who are lazy, drug-dealing absentee fathers and troublemakers. You have the potential to be whatever you want in life. The path to creating a solid, productive life begins with a healthy respect for yourself. Always believe in yourself, and be sold on your potential.

Respect for Our Women

Black women are worthy of your respect, and above that, need your respect. If you turn on the rap videos, black women are portrayed as sexual objects, not respect-deserving people. So many young women believe this imagery they are being fed about themselves from the music. The evidence is how they carry themselves, imitating the Nicki Minajes, Rihannas, and other overtly sexual female musical artists.

You don't have to be the guy going around disrespecting our black women and treating them as sexual objects. This is popular in young black male culture, but dare to be different by letting black women know their worth by treating them with respect at all times.

Many young black women might be attracted to the "bad boy" type, but believe me, she desires a solid black man she can build a life with. Become the solid black man a beautiful black woman can rely on to be her protector and partner for life.

Compliment your black woman, young brother. Tell her how beautiful she is. Be courteous to her. Open doors for her when you two go out. Help carry her belongings when you see her struggling.

Always walk on the outside of the sidewalk when you are out with her. This protects her from harm and lets her know you care about her well-being. Be a solid friend and mate she can confide in when she finds herself in difficult situations. Be the man who completes her.

Notes and Insights

Notes and Insights

Chapter 9: Choices

The ability to choose is a powerful gift. Your choices have the power to frame your world, for better or worse. The choices you are making today are creating your reality of tomorrow. The better the quality of your choices today, the brighter your future will be. Respect your ability to make choices. When you respect the gift of choice, when you understand the power choices have in shaping your life, you will automatically begin to make better ones.

Being intelligent with your choices is not making decisions until you've examined the outcome. Being a mature young male means that you think things through before you act. The devastation in our community is the result of youth making choices that aren't based on intelligently thinking about the outcome. Choices have many outcomes.

You harness the power to choose by weighing all outcomes before acting on your choices.

Success and Failure

Underneath it all, every choice you make is leading you closer to a life of success or failure. Look around at successful people, and people who have not been so successful. But when you look, I want you to see the deeper revelation of the choices they made in order to get to where they are in life.

Wisdom comes to us in the form of what is oftentimes not being said. When you examine the choices someone made with his or her life to be where he or she is, you are accessing unspoken wisdom. Wisdom does not always have to be someone telling you what to do. Wisdom can come from intelligently taking a hard look at someone else's life.

When I wanted to become a great athlete, I observed great athletes who had made it to places I wanted to be. The greatest advice I received was from the unspoken lessons I learned from the choices and routines of great athletes. When Kobe Bryant first entered the NBA, he was called names like "Carbon Copy Mike" and "Heir Jordan." These labels on Kobe Bryant came because it was obvious that he had observed every mannerism and habit of Michael Jordan, because he wanted to be just as great as, or better, than him. He observed him so much that he began to play like Mike, talk like Mike, and carry himself like Mike off the court.

Today, Kobe Bryant has surpassed Michael Jordan in some statistical categories, and is poised to pass him in even more. His legacy will be very close to that of Michael Jordan when he retires from the NBA. This is the result of him making the same choices Michael Jordan made to achieve a similar result.

When you look around you, understand that you can create the same outcomes others had with their lives by mimicking the choices they made. You don't just wake up one day and step into greatness. Being at the top of anything is accomplished through a continuous series of choices that eventually frame your world.

To the contrary, you don't just wake up one day as an adult and arrive at a place where you are "unsuccessful." This, too, is the result of a series of bad decisions that created a world of not being successful.

Allow life to teach you lessons every day. Be observant and learn to see what's not seen, and hear what's not heard, in terms of the good and bad outcomes of life, when you see them on display.

The Navigation System

Many new vehicles come standard with a navigation system that provides the driver with easy-to-follow directions on how to get anywhere in the United States. It makes the driving experience easier and more enjoyable, without the task of looking at a map or reading directions while attempting to drive.

What if I told you life has a navigation system? What if you could effortlessly observe the choices that have landed people where they are in life and train yourself to see the choices as being good or bad? If you continuously keep seeing people who are where you want to be, you will realize they made very similar choices to achieve very similar outcomes of success.

If you observe people who haven't quite been able to get it right in life, you will see a similar pattern of choices that are responsible for them being in their current condition.

When you train your mind to see the deeper meaning of the choices people make, and how they affect outcomes in life, the reasons behind the reality will be stuck in your mind. When it is stuck in your mind, whenever you are in a position where a choice needs to be made that affects your future, you are likely to make good decisions, based on the reality of the choices people had to make in order to get where they are in life.

This is how to mentally condition your mind to always make good choices, when you don't just look at people in their "here-and-now reality," but truly understand the choices that created their reality.

The Bigger Picture

Your choices don't just affect you; they impact everyone around you. If you do well in school, you make everyone around you happy as they sit in the stands at your graduation. If you hang around the wrong people and get caught on the wrong side of the law, people who care about you can sit in the courtroom at your sentencing. If you have a son or daughter who was just born, every choice you make is now going to affect the course of this child's life.

When we take off our selfish blinders in life, we can easily see the bigger picture of how our choices affect everyone around us, for better or worse. Successful choices and successful living make those around us proud, and affects them for the better. Poor choices, which often lead to bad consequences, make life a little harder on everyone around us, because they care. When someone cares about you, a large part of that person gets fulfillment when you do well. This same person experiences pain when you veer off the right path in life.

One of my turning points in life that helped me to get away from making bad choices was seeing my mother's smile on her face when I walked through the door. In an instant, I realized I had to make some serious changes, because I knew the devastation my mother would experience if my bad choices landed me in a prison, or worse, in a casket. I knew that if my choices caused me to lose my life, my mother would lose a large part of herself. Every day for the rest of her life without me would be that much more difficult because of my choices. Understand that life is bigger than just you.

We have to make so many choices on a daily basis, they can seem as if they don't carry much weight in determining outcomes for us. I titled this book ***Choices*** because no matter how much society places blacks at a disadvantage, we can overcome any adversity through the power of exercising choice effectively.

Here is an ideal set of choices I hope you make with your life. You have your fun and enjoy your youth. All the while, you are prioritizing your life in a way that places academics in a high position in your life. You take good care of your loved ones and do well to put smiles on their faces. You respect yourself and others and become a well-rounded young man. You graduate from high school and do whatever it takes to enroll in college. You stay focused and graduate from college. You use your intellect and college degree to navigate the world. You understand that a higher power of good is with you and will allow you to find your way, as you have always done. You create a successful adult life and help other young black males to do the same. This is my desire for you.

Prioritize Your Life

If you develop a vision for your life, and understand the power that choice plays in you achieving your vision, you will now naturally begin to prioritize your life. An awareness of choice and understanding, that they play a vital role in your success, means you must observe what's necessary to arrive at your vision. By understanding what is important, begin to prioritize your life in a way that will allow you to focus on what is important.

This may be new to you. If you never had a vision in life, and didn't understand the power of choice, you naturally wouldn't feel a need to prioritize your life. The power to choose means you have the power to change. If you want to see changes in your life, prioritize it in a way that encourages you to experience change. If you aren't where you want to be in life, understand that prioritizing your life differently gives you a fighting chance to experience the change you desire. If you are where you want to be, make changes to take you to an even higher realm of success. Our only job in life is to be who we uniquely are and never stop growing and changing. Choice is a powerful weapon.

Notes and Insights

Notes and Insights

Chapter 10: A Higher Reality

Throughout this book, I have discussed the reality of some of the challenges we face us young black men. With these difficulties being present, I introduced the solution of exercising your power to create the life you want for yourself in spite of many negative opinions that surround us. It may be overwhelming to think that you can shed the stereotypes of being young and black. My deep-seated belief and desire for you is that you always choose to hover in the lane of possibility, and never be afraid to create your vision in life.

This is possible when you realize that there is a higher reality than anything we could think of or imagine. What I'm talking about is the force that allowed you to win the race and be born. I am talking about the force of good that will aid you in your quest to live a successful, purposeful life, even when many in society think you can't.

Many people do not go after what they want from life because they have concerns about how and when everything will come together for them. Fear is a paralyzing force that keeps dreams stuck inside of people, instead of them turning them into realities as they have been empowered to do. The force of good will work with you as you take the steps to create the best life possible for you. Never worry about how and when your breaks will come in life. This statement is brought to life in the story below. You were created to experience breakthroughs in life if you choose not to quit when pursuing your desires.

As I am writing this book, a feverish buzz has emerged in the form of a basketball player named Jeremy Lin. He is an American-born Asian basketball player who rose to absolute prominence, from being repeatedly cut by NBA basketball teams, in the span of one week.

Jeremy Lin plays for the New York Knicks. They signed him from the NBA Development League, where he was playing because the Golden State Warriors recently had cut him from their team. This in-and-out double Dutch game of being in the NBA one day and being cut shortly thereafter was becoming routine for Lin in his short NBA career.

The New York Knicks were without their two superstars, Carmelo Anthony and Amar'e Stoudemire, who had been lost to injury and family death respectively. The Knicks had been struggling and headed toward not making the play-offs. They needed a spark, so the coach decided to give bench player, and NBA journeyman, Jeremy Lin a chance to start a game. His first game as the starting point guard, he scored twenty-eight points. His next start, he scored twenty-three points. His next start, he scored thirty-eight points against the Los Angeles Lakers while outscoring Kobe Bryant. His next game he scored twenty points. Each of these games resulted in a win for the Knicks, with Lin spearheading the way and being catapulted to stardom overnight.

Throughout his first five NBA starts, Jeremy Lin scored 189 points, which is the highest point total of any player during their first five NBA starts. He became an instant legend, and started a craze called "Linsanity." His moment of breakthrough came in an instant.

You couldn't watch television or listen to the radio during his historic run without hearing about Linsanity. In one of Lin's television interviews, he gave an explanation as to what was behind his sudden meteoric rise. His words go as follows: "This is a miracle, because many things had to happen for me to be in this position that are out of my control."

Fear is a paralyzing force that will keep you from exploring the possibilities of life. The possibilities of life are your dreams, desires, and most importantly, living the destiny you were created to live. Sometimes, as young black men, it can seem as if the deck is completely stacked against us. This feeling can be overwhelming, keeping you from even trying to create something greater for your life. There is an escape from this way of thinking, by choosing to believe in a force greater than you. Faith, in a very famous book, is described as "the substance of things hoped for, and evidence of things not seen."

Many times in life, the evidence isn't there to show you how your desires will happen. In spite of this, you must move toward your dreams. Jeremy Lin, in one of his interviews, described how he would go to sleep crying and praying that he wouldn't get cut from whatever team he was playing for. He had thoughts of giving up and finding a regular job. But he persevered. His reward is international stardom and the highest-selling jersey in the NBA.

The Power of Miracles

I repeatedly discuss our president, as his meteoric rise, and ultimate appointment as the president of the United States, was nothing short of a miracle. His presidential run took place at the height of the buzz from CNN's *Black in America*. Through CNN, America, independent of race, was able to get an in-depth look at life as a black man. The consensus still stands: Barack Obama's election was a miracle.

Imagine if our president worried about the outcome of his election when he decided to run for office? He would have never arrived at a place where he could entertain the possibility of him becoming the president of the Unites States. When you don't entertain the possibility of anything, it is over before you start.

It's a harsh reality to understand and experience life as a young black man. The reality becomes even more discouraging when CNN, the most trusted news source in the world, shows you these realities, with statistics to back them. This makes you see how serious of a challenge we face as young black men. Your saving grace in spite of it all is to focus on your Creator and understand that there is no outcome that is beyond His reach in life.

Choosing a higher reality simply means letting go of the fears that surround what you see and believing in a force that is greater than you. This force makes sure nature thrives, animals are taken care of, plants receive the rain they need to thrive, and that all of creation is taken care of in some form. If the force of good takes care of even the most miniscule of creatures on the planet, this force must deeply care about you, and not see your race, but the endless possibilities you possess as a human being.

There is no challenge you cannot overcome and no breakthrough you cannot experience. Don't sell yourself short in life by not pursuing your dreams. The fear of the outcome of how your dreams will happen can be overwhelming at times. But understand that outcomes are determined by something far greater than us, no matter how hard we work for something. Our job is to simply go after what we want in life, with no concern about outcomes.

If we could create outcomes, we wouldn't need a force bigger than us to serve as a guide through life, and open doors that lead to our destiny.

You may find yourself in a position where you need a miracle. Understand that miracles are possible for people who believe they can experience them. The two events I referred to in this chapter are indisputable miracles, given the realities they were up against. The same force that allowed these miracles to take place created you, and wants you to experience a life of breakthroughs and miraculous wonders.

I recently was watching a speech by famed playwright and movie producer Tyler Perry. His life is the essence of what a miracle is. He decided to begin producing plays as his first venture. In the beginning, he worked odd jobs, saving all of his money just to produce plays that few people would show up to. He was so dedicated to his vision that he even slept in his car so his money could be used to produce his plays.

He felt as if he was going nowhere, and that all of his efforts to get ahead were in vain. He talked about how he wanted to give up, but something inside of him simply wouldn't let him do it. In so many words, he was saying you are who you are. You have a destiny, and the force behind it is so strong it's difficult to give up even when you want to. What appeared on the path of Tyler Perry's journey was a miracle. He is now a mega-successful movie producer and playwright. He was one of Oprah Winfrey's favorite guests before her show went off the air. He is a worldwide phenomenon.

If he would not have followed his internal compass to keep going, he would have never met his miracle. I am urging you to keep going until you meet your miracle. We are all created by the same force, which has the ability to create breakthroughs and miracles for us, His most precious creation. Stay the course no matter what.

Just Do Your Job

Your job is to first not be intimidated by any dream or vision you have within yourself. You are then to pursue this vision with everything you have inside of you. From here, you keep on moving in spite of all fears and opposition you will face along the way. You are then free to allow your Creator to do His job, by creating the breakthroughs and miracles that have to take place to get you to your destinations in life.

If you choose to worry about outcomes, you are not doing your job. Worrying about outcomes is not in your job description. Do everything you can to experience the outcomes you want for yourself, and simply let that be that.

If you work toward something, and it is in line with your destiny, the breaks will come and create your desired outcome.

Please do not frustrate yourself by taking responsibility for something that you were never equipped to handle: creating outcomes.

There is a force of creation that has always existed, and will continue to exist for all eternity. This force is all-powerful, all-knowing, and has the final say in any earthly situation we will encounter. This power is what brought you into existence. This power created you with many gifts and talents, with the hopes that you would use them to chart a path in life. This force gave me the gift to speak words of life into you. This force has more power than any reality that is set before you as a young black man. This force will work with you, as you choose to do the right things in life, and create a positive impact in the world. This force will help you navigate your way through life.

This force guides you through a small voice from within. This force speaks to us in the form of desires that won't go away in spite of any realities we face. The desire that goes against the realities of life will happen, because the source of all creation possesses that level of power. CNN has their statistics, but there is none higher than this source.

Allow the voice from within to guide you through the highs and lows of life. I have found this voice to be the most helpful. When people told me I couldn't do things in life, I listened to the internal voice saying I could. Miracle after miracle has occurred in my life, and miracle after miracle can occur in yours as well. You are more than a young black man; you are an extension of the source of all creation. Society sees your race and views you with limitation. The source sees you simply as His creation, and has no boundaries regarding what you can become in life.

Your quality of life will depend on what reality you believe in the most: what this world says about you, or what the source of all creation has empowered you to do and be. There is a higher reality than what you can see. Always choose this reality over what you see, and you will elevate above all perceptions and misconceptions black men face.

You have unlimited brilliance, genius, and greatness. Believe.

Notes and Insights

Notes and Insights

About The Author

Matthew C. Horne, motivational speaker and author, is the president of Optimum Success International, a speaking and publishing company located in the metropolitan Washington, DC area. He is an international authority on Maximizing Human Potential. Matthew is the author of *The Universe Is Inviting You In,* and *All We Have Is NOW,* which are both publicly endorsed by legendary motivational speaker Les Brown. He is also the author of *Choices: The Young Black Man's Guide to Successful Living* and *How to Get Beautiful Women ....and Everything Else You Want From Life*. Growing up, Matthew's ultimate vision for his life was to play basketball in the NBA. He positioned himself to live this reality through obtaining a full-athletic scholarship to play Division I basketball in college. Much to his surprise destiny revealed his true calling during his collegiate years, as he discovered a passion for motivational speaking. Matthew was told by his professors he would never make it as an English major, and to the astonishment of everyone, he not only obtained a Bachelor of Arts Degree in English, but was offered his first book contract before he graduated in his last semester of college. Matthew's message is one of creating your own reality according your vivid destiny pictures. Matthew empowers audiences to live their unique truth, independent of the opinions of others. Matthew's message is quickly spanning the globe through his books, audios, and motivational speeches. He is a writer for the *Washington Post's* "The Root DC" section. He is a staff writer for *EmPower Magazine*. He is the co-host of the television show "How To Survive In A Bad Economy." He has also been featured on the legendary radio station WOL with his weekly minute motivational segments. Matthew is also a regular contributor to the internet's leading motivational ezine: Let's Talk Motivation. Matthew will bring any event to life! Matthew is available for speeches, radio and television interviews, and book signings. All who encounter Matthew C. Horne will leave with a heightened awareness of their limitless possibilities, and be positioned to live their Best Life Possible. To learn more about Matthew C. Horne, please visit www.matthewchorne.com.

Services

Motivational Speaking: Matthew C. Horne is the world's premier motivational speaker and leading authority in Maximizing Human Potential. His message has spanned the globe and will bring any audience to life through an awareness of their limitless possibilities and creative potential. Matthew is available for speeches, lectures, seminars, and radio and television interviews.

Testimonial:

Thank you very much for your recent motivational speech on "Peak Performance in the Workplace." I am very appreciative of what you delivered to our employees here at NASA Goddard Space Flight Center.

You brought your experience to the table and stressed teamwork. Your entire presentation was value-added. In a brief period of time, you stressed how employees can achieve peak performance by valuing their work and bringing their best work and attitude to everything they attempt.

—Michael P. Kelly
Chief, Institutional Support Office, NASA Goddard Space Flight Center

Also by Matthew C. Horne

Available at www.matthewchorne.com
$17.00 USD (ISBN: 978-0-9794550-0-1)

"The Universe is Inviting You In" is a great tool on the road to your destiny. Each of us must choose our path and utilize the knowledge and wisdom that is guiding our journey from within, giving us the power to live our dreams." Les Brown (The Motivator)

Available at www.matthewchorne.com

$17.00 USD (ISBN: 978-0-9794550-1-8)

"All We Have Is NOW...is a powerful guide which inspires us to rise to the occasion of being the great, creative and unstoppable beings that we were originally designed to be...offering valuable insights on how to leverage and build on the most precious moment set before us...NOW!"
Les Brown (The Motivator)

CPSIA information can be obtained
at www.ICGtesting.com
Printed in the USA
BVOW11s0821010817
490797BV00003B/16/P

9 780979 455025